I0022029

Get Paid to Take Digital Photos

Brenda Stephens

Contents

Disclaimer

Reasonable care has been taken to ensure that the information presented in this book is accurate. However, the reader should understand that the information provided does not constitute legal, medical or professional advice of any kind.

No Liability: this product is supplied "as is" and without warranties. All warranties, express or implied, are hereby disclaimed. Use of this product constitutes acceptance of the "No Liability" policy. If you do not agree with this policy, you are not permitted to use or distribute this product.

We shall not be liable for any losses or damages whatsoever (including, without limitation, consequential loss or damage) directly or indirectly arising from the use of this product.

Introduction

You're reading this because you have two passions in life. First, you love taking photos. You probably carry your camera everywhere with you, just waiting for a chance to snap a candid shot that tells a little story. That's the art of photography and, if you're reading this, you have a passion for that art.

But then there's your passion for money. Don't worry, you're not being judged. It's good to be motivated by money. It's what makes the world go 'round, right? Or is that love? Point is, money may not bring happiness, but it sure makes life a whole lot easier to get through.

And anyone knows that the best way to make money is to take what you love and turn it into a business. Well, congratulations. You have taken the first step towards making money doing what you love: Taking digital photos.

Not many people know that you can make a good living just by selling photos over the Internet. But once you become aware of just how many photos we're exposed to on a daily basis, the realization that you can make money taking great photos should be a no-brainer.

Photographs Everywhere You Look

You would have to live in a shack out in the woods like the Unabomber to not be exposed to literally hundreds of photographs per day. Think about your daily life. If you ate breakfast this morning, there was probably a picture of someone on the cereal box. If you made coffee, there might be a picture on the can, and that's just in your kitchen.

There are photos on the billboards as you drive to work. There are photos in the magazines when you sit in your dentist's waiting room, and you are bombarded with photos galore the moment you turn on your computer and start browsing the Internet.

The point is, every industry needs photographs. And while there are many experts out there who get paid very handsomely for the photographs they churn out (think major magazine photographers), amateurs are able to make great money doing what they love, too!

That's right. You don't have to be a professional. You can go out right now, pick up a digital camera and you can theoretically start making money off of those photographs. And I'm going to show you how.

First, however, before you rush out thinking you're the next Annie Leibovitz, you need to consider if you have what it takes to make money from your photos.

That can be a hard thing to ascertain, especially when you have a passion for something. Because the truth is, you could enthusiastically take loads and loads of pictures but there's no guarantee that any of them will sell.

To fail at something you love to do can hurt deep down in your core. But you must remember that just because your photo doesn't sell, doesn't mean you're no good. It could be for a number of reasons.

The point is to have patience, and make sure you learn how it's done before you start selling your photos for money.

Once you're done reading this, you'll have all the tools you need to get started. Only then will you truly see the potential for making money that's eluded you all this time because you never took the time to wonder where all the photos you're surrounded with daily actually come from.

Do You Have What it Takes?

If you think it's easy to sell digital photos online, you're mistaken. Show me one person who's made it big selling photos, and I'll show you ten more just like him/her that don't make squat. They could even be taking pictures of the same things. The difference between them is that the person who made it put time and effort into his/her photo business. So ask yourself, do you have what it takes to sell your digital photos online?

If you said yes, then you must commit yourself if you hope to make it.

Go back and read that sentence again. That's the most important aspect of making money through digital photography. You must put in the required time and you must remain passionate about what you're doing because that passion, or lack of it, will come out in your photos. And finally, you must be able to have patience until you've learned enough to actually know which photos will sell, and which ones won't.

Time

The amount of money you make with your photos depends on how much time you invest in your business. On average, you should expect to work at least four hours per week, and more if you're really ambitious. Four hours is nothing and it's worth it when you consider you're doing what you love.

Are You Creative?

This is a huge one. You can take a thousand pictures of your cat and it's likely not one of them will sell for even a penny. That's because cats have been done. You need to step out of your immediate surroundings, get out of your comfort zone, and you need to think outside the box.

Carry your camera with you wherever you go and be on the lookout for an image that just screams, "Take my picture!". This could be a shard of ice hanging from a lighthouse bridge. It could be a neighborhood dog catching a Frisbee, or it could be the way the sunset splashes vivid colors across the darkened sky.

Equipment

Obviously, if you're going to sell digital photos, you're going to need a digital camera. But to increase your chances of making a sale, you might want to invest in a few other things, as well.

The camera is number one. You must have a digital camera. There are many on the market these days and most of them produce excellent quality photographs. The prices are dropping on them all the time, so you should be able to get a decent one for cheap.

But what about editing software? Have you considered that you may want to doctor your photos so that they come out absolutely perfect? Do you know how to use that editing software to its fullest potential? Finally, do you even know how to take good photos?

These are all questions you really need to consider before you try your hand at this lucrative but competitive business.

There is a lot of money to be made, but there's also beautiful photography to be made, as well. It really is a great way to earn a living. It's fun, and there's just something fulfilling knowing that others are willing to pay for the photos you've taken. However, you must also be ready to deal with rejection - because that can be the most difficult part of this whole business.

Rejection

You may find that you're in love with your photos, but that you're the only one who feels that way. It's kind of like when someone brings along their dog and they go on and on about how cute and loveable their dog is, but everyone else doesn't feel that way. Some people may be allergic to dogs. The dog may be lovable but that doesn't mean they want to risk touching it so they'll blow up like a balloon.

The point is, you can't please everybody. If you take a beautiful photograph and nobody likes it, don't let it get you down. Those people just don't have good taste, that's all. Or they don't need that photograph for any particular reason.

See, most people buy photos because they're looking for a particular one. They may need a butterfly photo for a website, or a doctor photo for a brochure. Part of this business is making sure your photos get seen by the right people, but we'll get into that later.

You must be able to deal with rejection or else you'll never make it in the photography business. If you don't make any sales, just keep doing what you're doing and give it time. You must have patience until your efforts begin to pay off.

Work day by day, little by little, and before you know it you'll know what it takes to sell photos online and you'll have done it from pure knowledge and hard work.

So if by now you've decided that you have what it takes to sell your digital photos online, let's get started.

Choosing a Camera

If you don't already have a camera, you know you need one. But you're likely going to find a lot of choices out there. There are so many different types of cameras, brands and accessories that it can seem almost overwhelming. However, picking out a good camera isn't that difficult at all.

Simply get online and start researching the cameras you come across based on a few criteria. You'll want to be focused on the amount of megapixels the camera has, as well as the quality of the sensor. But of course price is going to be an issue, as well. So your job is to find a camera that offers the most for the least amount of money. That sounds obvious, but it's not easy when you're bombarded by so many different types of digital cameras.

However, there are a couple ways you can go about getting a camera that's of good enough quality to take excellent photographs.

Experts

If you want to know something about a subject, you turn to an expert, right? In keeping with that same thinking, camera experts are who you should turn to when you're trying to find the perfect camera for you.

You can find experts online on consumer report websites, or you can read reviews by experts that are posted online. You can also ask clerks that work in the camera sections of your favorite stores. These employees spend all day looking at, talking about, and learning about digital cameras. Ask them plenty of questions and tell them what you're trying to do.

You will want to make sure that the camera you choose is at least a 5 megapixel camera. Remember that just because the megapixel count is high, doesn't mean the photos are going to be better. Make sure the sensor is of high quality, as well.

Most people find that cameras where you are able to change the lenses produce better quality images, but you should be fine with your everyday run-of-the-mill digital camera.

Digital Photo Editing

If you don't know how to properly edit a photograph, you're starting out with a huge disadvantage. You may think that digital editing is cheating. After all, the photo should be sold based on the natural beauty of the image captured. There should be no editing going on. If it's not in the photo, then you shouldn't be paid for it.

There are a lot of old timers stuck in their ways that still hold onto that idea. But the fact is, every industry uses digital editing to enhance photography.

Programs like Photoshop and other digital editing software allow you to do all sorts of things to enhance a photograph in order to prime it for sale. Not only can you take the red out of someone's eyes, but you can crop, change colors, change an object's density, create shadow detail, and that's just to name a few.

So if you don't know how to use any of the common programs out there for editing the photographs you take, it's recommended that you get one so that you can stay abreast or ahead of the competition who will surely be using it.

And now, the issue of money.

Get 'Get Rich Quick' Out of Your Head

It doesn't matter what the subject is, someone's figured out a way for you to get rich quick. They explain it to you in detail and they may even sell you an eBook or a report, or even a video, and you buy it, only to find out that the tactics don't work. Do you know how many people have actually gotten rich quick from all of the get rich quick programs out there? Less than 2%!

And the ones that do make it have a lot of free time and a lot of luck. Now don't get me wrong. You can make money selling your digital photos online. You just have to remain realistic about your goals.

Making money in anything takes time. You may have to start at the bottom, but soon, after enough hard work, you can make it to the middle. Then, if you're really ambitious, you can climb all the way to the top.

Nothing is going to be handed to you and you're going to get rejected (a lot) and you're likely not going to make much when you first start out. You're going to have to build a solid foundation, which is learning as much as you can about the trade, and then build on that foundation with more education and hard work. Eventually you'll become proficient enough that you'll be able to spot those winning photographs and that's when you'll start making good money.

It could take six weeks, it could take six months and it could even take a couple of years. But if this is something you really want to do, you'll do whatever it takes to become as good at it as possible.

Of course, there are exceptions.

Like Winning the Lottery

Although it's unlikely, you can always hold out for the hope that you'll get that one winning photograph that takes the world by storm. You know the photos I'm talking about. These are the ones that either touch people deeply, or they're so funny that people can't wait to share them with others. These are the photos that end up making the most amounts of money. But taking a photograph like this is akin to winning the lottery. It's not a safe bet, in other words.

The photos that make the most money include those taken of celebrities, funny candid photos and even heart wrenching photos like the one of the fireman holding the injured child right after the Oklahoma City Bombings.

While it is possible to take a photo that could potentially make you hundreds of thousands of dollars or more, it's best not to focus on photographs like those.

Instead, focus on the photos that you think are good. Take enough of them and you'll build a reputation. Get enough people to buy your photos and your sale record will begin to speak for itself. But all of this takes time to build. As long as you're consistent, and you put in the required effort, you'll be able to sell as many photos as you want, and you'll make some good money in the process.

You aren't going to get rich, at least not right away. You have to get good if you hope to make enough money so that you never have to work again, which, for paid photography, is very possible.

Now that we have that settled, and now that you've set some realistic goals, let's find out how to sell the photos you've taken so that you can start on your photo selling journey.

Microstock Photography

You may have heard of stock photography. This is where an image is licensed to be used by a specific person for a specific reason. For instance, a webmaster may need a certain type of photo for a website. Instead of risking taking one off the Internet and getting into copyright issues once the site becomes successful, the webmaster decides to buy the image so that he can use it legally.

Stock agencies are typically very picky about who they accept as photographers. So if you don't have that much experience, but you're still excited with the concept of making money with your photos, you'll be happy to know that an offshoot of stock photography exists on the Internet. This is known as microstock photography.

Microstock photography sites encourage professionals, amateurs and hobbyists alike to submit their photos for sale. These sites get almost all of their photos from individuals just like you, and they're also known for their low prices. That's both good and bad news for you.

The good news is that the low prices mean that customers are likely to keep coming back for more. You could form a long relationship with a client who loves your work and can only afford to pay the nominal fee the site charges for your photos. Now, consider if the same client had to pay hundreds of dollars for a photo. You may not see that client again after that, unless your reputation preceded you.

These microstock sites typically charge anywhere from $.20 to $10.00. While that may not seem like much money, it adds up if you're a good enough photographer and you're able to sell a lot of photos.

Selling your photos on these sites sounds great, doesn't it? All you have to do is take the photo and the site does the selling for you. Believe me, this is much better than taking your photos and trying to sell them yourself. While you can make more money doing your own marketing and selling, you're likely going to put in a whole lot more time than you make in dollars. It would be best to use one of these sites until you're good enough to venture out on your own.

Now, let's take a look at some of these microstock photography sites so that you can decide which one(s) to use.

Sites that Pay for Your Photos

Now that you have a camera and you're ready to publish them online so that you can make some money, it's time to find some microstock sites to add your photos to.

You'll find that some sites pay more than others, and you'll also find a variation in the pay terms as well as methods of payment. Hopefully, this guide will help you choose one that's right for your needs.

Shutterstock

This microstock site can be extremely lucrative, but first you have to be accepted. The main complaint you may hear about Shutterstock is that they're picky about who they accept for their site. To get accepted, you must send in ten photos and have at least seven of them accepted by a review team.

It's important to understand how stock photography works, and you also must have good equipment. It's not uncommon to have to try a few times before getting accepted on this site. But if you can get in, the income potential is quite high.

Dreamstime

This microstock site has a proven track record and it gets many visitors per day, as well as many sales. When you submit your photos to Dreamstime, you stand to make 50% commission on each sale you make. The best part is that you don't have to send any test photos in order to get accepted. So this might be a good site to start with until you get a little more experience.

It must be stated that even though they accept unknown photographers, they do check all of the images they receive and they will reject any photos that they deem are of a lower quality.

Fotolia

Fotolia is sort of new on the microstock scene. They are quickly gaining popularity, however, and they have customers that span the globe. Fotolia isn't known for its high commissions but your prices can go up once you gain through the ranks and get more sales.

The single most heard complaint about Fotolia, besides their long upload time, is the fact that they have a blacklist which includes all photos they no longer need. If you shoot a lot of horse photos, for instance, you may find that the site is saturated with them and that horses are now on that list.

Shutterstock, Dreamstime and Fotolia are the main microstock sites that most people use to successfully sell their photos. However, new sites are popping up all the time.

When choosing a site, make sure you're dealing with a legitimate site. Whenever something becomes popular on the Internet, such as making money by taking digital photos, it seems that crooks and scam artists can't wait to capitalize on poor, unwitting individuals who just want to make a few bucks using their passion and talent.

So check out all the sites you're considering before you register. Check user reviews, really look at the site's operations and make sure you will be paid when your photos do indeed sell.

Maximize Earnings

The ideal move for anyone who is serious about making money through selling their digital photos is to submit your photos to any sites you come across. That way you stand to get much more exposure, and it also allows you to test different photos to see which ones people like the most across several different platforms.

Before you register for these sites and begin posting your photos, you need to know how to market your photos, how to make them attractive for buyers, and you need to know what photos to take.

Once you learn the process of selecting the right photos, and marketing them so that buyers can't turn them down, you'll be able to experience the joy that comes from selling the photos that you took with your vision, your passion and your own hard work.

So, what process should you follow? How can you make sure that your photos sell the most? It's a tricky process, but it's not hard once you get the hang of it. It's all about viewing your photos through the customer's eyes.

Posting Your Photos Online

When you post your photos online, you are essentially offering them forever. Whatever you sell, you give up the rights to. For some, that's hard to do, especially if they are really in love with the photo they've taken.

For others, they consider they're getting paid so the idea of losing the rights hurts that much less. That's why they're doing this, after all. They're taking photos to make money.

Pricing

The hardest decision you're going to make when posting your photos on these microstock websites is how much to charge for each photo. There is no easy answer to this. How much you charge for your photos essentially relies on a few factors: 1) How long you've been a photographer. 2) How many photos you've sold. And 3) How good is the photo in question?

These are the questions people are going to ask themselves when they consider buying your photos. So you had better think about those answers when deciding on what to charge for each photo.

For instance, even if you took a photo that you're completely proud of, if you are a beginner and you don't have any sales credits to your name, customers likely won't spend a lot of money on your collection.

On the other hand, if you keep at it, eventually your photos will get better and better and, because of your extra experience and sales, you'll be able to charge much higher prices so that you can actually earn some good money.

So make sure you start small at first. Customers will be more willing to take a chance on you if your prices are very small. Just do your best, and always bring quality, so that you can change your prices to something more favorable later on.

Sell Your Photos!

If you want to become good at selling photos, you must study those who are successful. Most of these sites will allow you to investigate the photos that are most in demand, the ones that have sold the most, and the ones that are desperately needed. This information can give you the hints you need to know what to go out and shoot.

Your Target Audience

When you take a photo with the intent of selling it, sometimes it helps to picture your target audience. Those are the customers who buy your work. What do they typically look for? What sorts of images do they request or regularly buy? What angles do they prefer? What prices do they usually pay?

By knowing your target audience, you'll be better prepared to give them what they want and you'll double your chances of making sales.

Some would say that tailoring your shots according to what the clients want takes away from the beauty and candidness that makes up the art of photography. But don't newspaper and magazine reporters do that all the time? What about the Paparazzi? They're all photographers who set out to make money with their photographs and they're giving the consumers what they want.

And that's exactly what you're doing with these microstock websites. You're providing a service. That service just happens to be something you're skilled at creating. So they pay you accordingly. Get good enough and you'll never have to go back to an office job again.

Search for Information and Ask Questions

You can really get ahead of the game if you seek out one of the microstock forums where experts and amateurs alike gather to share tips and tricks of the trade. These forums can not only be a great platform for advertising your art, but you can also learn a lot about the entire process so that you can improve over time.

These forums are also great places to ask about which sites are best for your time and money. You may find that a lot of members have had a problem with one of the sites paying on time. That's helpful information for anyone looking for a microstock site to join so that they can begin their photo selling venture.

Who Buys Photos?

It's important to think of yourself as the customer. Think about the industry he or she is in. Think of the photo they'd need for their…whatever. Understanding your customers' needs is the first step towards producing the quality work they're willing to pay good money for.

Who needs photos? The majority of industries require photos for a number of reasons. Web designers need them for the websites they design for clients, businesses need them for marketing purposes and the media thrives on good photos to highlight news stories. The people who buy these photos want to ensure the photos they use are unique and original and so they pay money to ensure that's the case. That's where you come in.

Magazine editors obviously need photos. If you can sell a photo to a magazine, depending on how big it is, it can be a very nice payday. Capture that one candid shot that no other photographer can and you could find yourself holding a jackpot in your hands.

But the list goes on and on. Graphic artists, advertisers, affiliates, scrap bookers, teachers, lawyers, realtors, illustrators, chefs, travel agents, etc. etc.

The fact is, there will never cease to be a demand for good photos. Photos capture time in perfect clarity. They are the closest thing we have to a time machine. Advertisers and marketers know that the proper photos can create a bond with the customer and can make them feel more at ease about buying whatever they happen to be selling.

So you're always going to be able to sell your photos as long as these sites exist.

Of course, there are other ways to make money selling your digital photos, but these require a little more legwork on your part.

For the Truly Ambitious

If you are really confident in your photography skills, and you know that you can produce the kind of work that people will be willing to pay top dollar for, there are quite a few avenues you can pursue. For instance, you could become a wedding photographer, which gets paid very handsomely I might add.

Magazines pay very well, and so do newspapers. The bottom line is that if you can take really good photographs, and you're sure they have a market, you should do anything in your power to make that dream of living off your art a reality.

While using the tips and tricks in this book, keep reading up on those forums and educate yourself as much as possible. Put ads in the newspaper and online, such as on Craigslist. Advertise your skills and tell people where to go online to see samples of your work.

On the microstock websites, really take care to make your photos look as professional as possible. Make sure you price them according to the parameters we set earlier. The only exception to that rule is if you think you can command a higher price, because sometimes that can come out in your favor.

When people see that a particular piece is priced higher than all the others, it can make them stop and wonder why that piece is as high as it is. What is it about that photo that's different than all the others? This is one of the ways you cause hype, and that's how you can sell more photos.

So, to recap, get a good camera, get out there and take some of the most beautiful, breathtaking photos you've ever taken and then find one of the many microstock sites out there. Or, if your photos are good enough, submit them to the stock photo sites. You never know what can happen.

Once your photos are up, price them accordingly and keep taking more photos. Keep adding photos to your profile. Even if you're not selling, keep shooting and posting anyway.

Pay attention to those photos that are really selling and learn from them. Find out how to create those photos that have people demanding them. The knowledge is out there and people are using it to make lots of money doing what they love.

So get out there and do what you love. Be patient and be vigilant and soon you'll be able to live off your art. Hurry, your audience is waiting.

www.ingramcontent.com/pod-product-compliance
Lightning Source LLC
Chambersburg PA
CBHW071554080326
40690CB00056B/2034